CW00375675

Pocket Prayers
for Parents

Other books in the series:

Pocket Celtic Prayers
compiled by Martin Wallace

Pocket Graces
compiled by Pam Robertson

Pocket Prayers
compiled by Christopher Herbert

Pocket Prayers for Children
compiled by Hamish and Sue Bruce

Pocket Prayers for Healing and Wholeness
compiled by Trevor Lloyd

Pocket Prayers for Marriage
compiled by Andrew and Pippa Body

Pocket Words of Comfort
compiled by Christopher Herbert

Pocket Prayers
for Parents

COMPILED BY
Hamish and Sue Bruce

CHURCH HOUSE
PUBLISHING

Church House Publishing
Church House
Great Smith Street
London SW1P 3NZ
Tel: 020 7898 1451
Fax: 020 7898 1449

ISBN 0 7151 4019 1

Published 2004 by Church House Publishing

Typeset by Vitaset, Paddock Wood, Kent
Printed in England by the University Printing House,
Cambridge

CONTENTS

DEDICATED TO OUR SONS DAVID AND
JONATHAN AND TO GORDON AND ROSEMARY,
VICTOR AND DOROTHY, WHO CONTINUE TO BE
OUR SHINING EXAMPLES OF PARENTHOOD.

INTRODUCTION

Being a parent is one of the greatest challenges
that we face in life.

   We are parents of two boys – David, aged 10
and Jonathan, aged 8. When David was born
we were both teachers who were used to dealing
with children in a professional role. Yet it really
struck us how different the role of the parent is
and the many challenges and joys that it brings.

   As parents there are many opportunities to
pray with, or for our children, whether in
offering up 'arrow prayers' in times of stress,
giving thanks for our child, or praying with
them at mealtimes or bedtimes. In this book of
Pocket Prayers for Parents we have tried to
bring together a mixture of traditional and
contemporary prayers, for parents to use
'in all times and in all places'.

   We hope that these prayers will be useful on
various occasions, from the trepidation of facing
parenthood for the first time, through to letting
go of our children when they leave home.

Hamish and Sue Bruce

CHANGING LIFE (NEW PARENTS)

Becoming a parent for the first time – whether through the birth of a child, or welcoming a child by adoption – brings so many changes. We certainly found this for ourselves, coinciding also with a new job and lots of travelling – so life was fairly hectic anyway. The months of pregnancy are full of excitement, yet also plenty of trepidation. Then the longed for baby arrives and you realize this new member of your family is here to stay and demands plenty of attention! However 'good' you may be with babies or children, it is always a steep learning curve. We hope the prayers in this section will echo some of the feelings of new parents as they rejoice in their new baby and adjust to each other in their new role as parents.

*

Prayer of a New Mother

Creator God,
You created life and it was good.
And now I have new life in my arms.
Thank you for the privilege of being part
   of your creative self.
Thank you for the miracle of birth.
Thank you for my baby,
   such a perfect tiny being
with a future stretching before him.
So many questions, fears, hopes
   and dreams.
Lord, help me to bring to you
   the questions,
trust you through the fears
and offer to you the hopes and dreams
that this life you created through me
might be good.

Sue Bruce

For a New Father

Loving God,
As I hold my baby in my arms
I feel overwhelmed by a mixture
    of emotions –
of love and pride at the birth of such an
    amazing, beautiful child,
but also fear that I won't be able to cope
    with all the challenges of the future.
Help me, Lord, to trust in your unfailing
    love to help me when my patience fails
and to face each new challenge with the
    knowledge that you are with me now,
just as you have been since my father held
    me in his own arms.

Hamish Bruce

✳

Prayers Before the Birth

PRAYER FOR THE MOTHER-TO-BE

Living God, we thank you for your
    gracious invitation to share in the gift
    of creation.
Bless ... as she approaches the time for the
    delivery of her *baby/babies*.
In your compassion, give her strength to
    endure the pain she will feel in the
    bringing forth of a new life.
Protect both her and her *child/children*
    from harm and grant them a safe
    passage through the exertions of labour.
Grant that soon they may rest together,
    rejoicing in one another and in your
    love for them through Jesus Christ,
    our Lord.
Amen.

Janet Henderson from *Pastoral Prayers*

PRAYER FOR THE FATHER-TO-BE

Lord Jesus Christ, who shared the pains of
a human life, wait with us as we wait with
… (*mother's name*). Bring her relief during
her labour and grant that … (*father's
name*) may soon know that the pains
of birth have not been in vain as he and
… share the joy of seeing their child.
Amen.

Janet Henderson from *Pastoral Prayers*

A Mother's Psalm

Give praise for the gift of children,
for the birth of love
and the blessings of laughter and joy and
　　rollicking music.
Sing out to God,
who from the shadows of pain
gives birth to life anew.
Celebrate.
For with the ravines and lonely valleys
comes the warm wind
and the life-giving rain.

Sierra Leone

For Parents of Young Children

Father, in the life we have received
    from you,
you have given us the power to create
    new life,
a seed sown in love that becomes a child
    who is part of us.
For the awesome joy of that gift,
thank you, Father.
For the energetic, inquisitive, mirthful,
    messy, unpredictable delights
    of childhood,
thank you, Father.
For those who find joy in their children and
    are faithful in their parenthood,
thank you, Father.

Michael Walker

*

The Mother's Blessing

Where thou shalt bring the crown of thy head,
　Where thou shalt bring the tablet
　　of thy brow,
Strength be to thee therein,
　Blest be to thee the powers therein;
　Strength be to thee therein;
　Blest be to thee the powers therein.

Lasting be thou in thy lying down,
　Lasting be thou in thy rising up,
Lasting be thou by night and day,
　And surpassing good be heaven
　　to my dear one;
　Lasting be thou by day and by day,
　And surpassing good be heaven
　　to my dear one.

The face of God be to thy countenance,
The face of Christ the kindly,
The face of the Spirit Holy
　Be saving thee each hour
　In danger and in sorrow:
　　Be saving thee each hour
　　In danger and in sorrow.

A Celtic Prayer

Sleepless Nights

Watch thou, O Lord,
with those who wake, or watch,
    or weep tonight,
and give thine angels charge over those
    who sleep.
Tend thy sick ones, O Lord Christ;
rest thy weary ones;
bless thy dying ones;
soothe thy suffering ones;
pity thine afflicted ones;
shield thy joyous ones,
and all for thy love's sake.

St Augustine (354–430)

✳

Help me, God.
I'm so tired I can no longer give this child
    the attention she deserves.
All I want is a good night's sleep.
But she wants my love, my care, my touch,
    my attention.
Help me to be patient when all I want to
    do is to run away.
Help me to have strength to last through
    this night.

Hamish Bruce

For the care of mothers;
Thanks be to God.

For their patience when tested;
Thanks be to God.

For their love when tired;
Thanks be to God.

For their hope when despairing;
Thanks be to God.

For their service without limit;
Thanks be to God.

New Patterns for Worship

Birth of a Brother or Sister

Jesus, you grew up in an earthly family and
    had brothers.
How did you feel, I wonder, when it was
    no longer just Mary, Joseph and you?
We pray for ... as we welcome a new baby
    into our family.
Please give us wisdom and sensitivity
    as parents.
Please reassure ... of our love and your
    love for them, as a unique and
    irreplaceable person.
And may we grow closer together through
    the birth of our new baby.

Sue Bruce

Changed Relationship with Partner

God of our human forms and frailty
in whose love we are created
create in me a new love.
A love that savours the touch
of the husband who gave me a child.
From a relationship that felt complete
    with two,
create space for the two to become three.
And never let the original bond weaken.
Give our partnering a new potential
for deeper, all-the-more-knowing intimacy.
Amen.

Ali Lawrence

✳

Give me grace Lord
to welcome the differences
in my wife who is now a 'survivor'
of the struggle to give birth
and whose body so quickly
becomes nourishing softness to our baby.
Amen.

Chris Lawrence

Prayer for Life Changes

Dear Lord,
Please help me not to lose who I am in
these changes.
Help me to remember that you love me,
that you care about me and that in the
midst of all this
you are actually working things out the
best for me.
Help me to guard against resentment
and loneliness.
Help me to believe that you haven't
abandoned me.
Help me to learn from all this and to see
you in places
I would never normally see you.
Help me to understand that you are
training me for something
and to believe that, in time, all this will
make sense.
I don't want to lose you Lord,
keep hold of me,
I'm hanging on to you.
Amen.

Cathy Silman

We thank thee, God, for the moments
    of fulfilment:
the end of a hard day's work,
the harvest of sugar cane,
the birth of a child,
for in these pauses,
we feel the rhythm of the eternal.
Amen.

Prayer from Hawaii

Christening

We thank you, Father God, for creating
    the beautiful world we live in
and for filling it with signs of your love
    and glory.

We thank you, Lord Jesus, for coming to
    live, and die and rise among us,
showing us the way to the Father.

We thank you, Holy Spirit, for your work
    in our lives and hearts,
changing us and working through us,
    making us more like Jesus.

Today we thank you especially for your gift
    to us of these children.
Thank you for your love for them, and
    your good purposes for them.

We ask that the whole of their lives would
    be a journey deeper into your love.
We ask that any hurts they have known
    will be healed,
and your blessing will rest upon them.
We ask that they will be filled with your
    Spirit, and that they will grow in
    knowledge of you.

Pam Macnaughton

Baptism

May God, who has received you by
    baptism into his Church,
pour upon you the riches of his grace,
that within the company of Christ's
    pilgrim people
you may daily be renewed
    by his anointing Spirit,
and come to the inheritance of the saints
    in glory.
Amen.

Common Worship

❋

God of grace and life,
in your love you have given us
a place among your people;
keep us faithful to our baptism,
and prepare us for that glorious day
when the whole creation will be made perfect
in your Son our Saviour Jesus Christ.
Amen.

Common Worship

DURING THE DAY

Some people might remember prayers their own parents used with them, particularly at mealtimes or bedtimes. As children grow up, there are opportunities throughout each day to pray for them and with them, as they live through various rituals and experiences – from that manic 'getting ready for school' time, through to the bedtime routine. We have included both traditional prayers and contemporary ones, which we hope will be relevant and useful through each day. Some of these are 'responsive' prayers, with an older child or parent leading the prayer and the rest of the family saying the text in **bold type.**

The Lord is with us, he is our stronghold;
God will help at the break of day.
The Lord is with us, he is our stronghold;
God will help at the break of day.

God is our refuge and strength,
ready to help whenever we are in trouble:
God will help at the break of day.

We will not fear, even if the earth shakes,
and the mountains topple into the sea:
God will help at the break of day.

Come now and look at the works of the Lord,
the awesome things he has done on earth:
God will help at the break of day.

Be still and know that I am God;
I will be exalted among the nations;
I will be exalted in the earth:
God will help at the break of day.

Glory to the Father, and to the Son, and to
the Holy Spirit.
The Lord is with us, he is our stronghold:
God will help at the break of day.

Psalm 46.1-3,8,10
New Patterns for Worship

God with me lying down,
God with me rising up,
God with me in each ray of light,
Nor I a ray of joy without him,
   Nor one ray without him.

Christ be with me sleeping,
Christ be with me waking,
Christ be with me watching,
Every day and night,
   Each day and night.

God with me protecting,
The Lord with me directing,
The Spirit with me strengthening,
For ever and evermore,
   Ever and evermore, Amen.
   Chief of chiefs, Amen.

Carmina Gadelica

Through every minute of this day,
be with me, Lord!
Through every day of all this week,
be with me, Lord!
Through every week of all this year,
be with me, Lord!
Through all the years of all this life,
be with me, Lord!
So shall the days and weeks and years
be threaded on a golden cord.
And all draw on with sweet accord
unto thy fullness, Lord,
that so, when time is past,
by grace I may at last
be with thee, Lord.

John Oxenham (1853–1941)

Here, Lord, is my life.
I place it on the altar today.
Use it as you will.

Albert Schweitzer (1875–1965)

Lord, make me an instrument
    of your peace:
where there is hatred,
    let me bring your love;
where there is injury, pardon;
where there is discord, union;
where there is doubt, faith;
where there is despair, hope;
where there is darkness, light;
where there is sadness, joy;
for your mercy's sake.

Attributed to St Francis of Assisi (1182–1226)

Getting Children Ready in the Morning

Lord, I'm going to scream.

I am going to count up to ten and scream.
One ...
I missed my vocation in life. I should have
    been a tape recorder!
'Pack your homework', ' Where's your PE
    kit?' ...

Two, three ...
'If I have to tell you again, stop dreaming,
    lunch box'.

Four ...
Lord, I'm not joking,

Five ...
Every day the same, I'm sick of shouting,
    give me strength.

Six – calm, breathe, Seven ...
'What are you doing today? Worried about
    anything? Give Mummy a kiss.

Eight ... Nine
Bye bye, see you later
Quiet, so quiet.

Thank you Lord
She's wonderful.

Mark Ripley

Getting Children Ready — Before the Rush

Thank you for my child.
For letting him be with us
     these few short years.
Sometimes it's so frantic,
     so tiring that I forget.

I forget the women who cry every day
     because they're not mothers.
I forget that one day I will be old and these
     will be golden years.
Grant me the patience and grace to make
     the memories well.
Amen.

Mark Ripley

Loving Father
As we walk to school, hold her other hand,
And when I let her go, keep your hold.
May she know your loving presence
     at her side,
At school and as you lead us both home.

Ros Hughes

Christ be with me, Christ within me,
Christ behind me, Christ before me,
Christ beside me, Christ to win me,
Christ to comfort and restore me,
Christ beneath me, Christ above me,
Christ in quiet, Christ in danger,
Christ in hearts of all that love me,
Christ in mouth of friend and stranger.

St Patrick (5th century)

God to enfold me,
    God to surround me,
God in my speaking,
    God in my thinking.

God in my sleeping,
    God in my waking,
God in my watching,
    God in my hoping.

God in my life,
    God in my lips,
God in my soul,
    God in my heart.

Carmina Gadelica

Lord, this is harder than I ever imagined!
Thought I'd be one of those super-mums
Sorting all the emails between feeds
Blitzing the house once she sleeps
Getting the visiting done en route
    to the shops
(all when she's happy, of course!).
Instead, I can't seem to sleep enough
    or cry enough
or DO enough
to enjoy it.
Help me please,
You who mothered and fathered me,
    your child
with relentless patience and care.
Help me to have enough for my child,
Just enough of whatever it takes.
Amen.

Ali Lawrence

Lord, you know how hard I can find these
    days at home with my child
From the early morning waking
Through the long hours of the day,
Playing the sometimes rather tedious games
Doing that puzzle again
    for the hundredth time
And still trying to sound excited as you fit
    the last piece in,
Encouraging them to eat, and not minding
    if half the carefully prepared meal ends
    up on the floor.
The trips to the playground and having to
    push on swings, bounce on seesaws,
    persuade along climbing frames.
The lack of stimulation and adult
    communication.
Right through to the splashing bath time and
    bedtime story and cuddle – I love that bit!
Lord, help me to have patience and to
    appreciate these times.
I know I will look back with nostalgia on
    them in a few years.
Please make me more grateful
And may lasting bonds be forged between
    my child and me through these days.

Sue Bruce

School Events

Inside this school, O Lord,
    there are lots of people
trying to know and understand your world.
Give us courage when things are difficult,
hope when things seem gloomy
and joy when things go well.

Christopher Herbert

God bless our school;
bless those who teach,
bless those who learn,
and bless us all with the knowledge
    of your love;
through Jesus Christ our Lord.

Christopher Herbert

Weekend Events

O Lord
As we stand shivering on the sidelines
     yet again
Thank you
For the enthusiasm of our children,
For the commitment of their teachers,
For the place to be and the homes to go to.
Amen.

Mary Langshaw

✳

Mealtimes

The bread is pure and fresh,
The water cool and clear.
Lord of all life be with us,
Lord of all life be near.

African Grace

✳

We thank you, Father, God of love,
for the signs of your love on this table,
for your love made known through
    all the world
and shining on us in the face of Jesus
    Christ, our Lord.
Amen.

The Promise of His Glory

I have heard that as many people in the
    world are overnourished
    as undernourished.
I have heard that the number of people
    living alone is rising.
Help us Lord, to eat well and with care.
    To make our meals a celebration
    of our lives together. To sometimes
    include the lonely in what we can
    so easily take for granted.
Amen.

Mark Ripley

Bedtimes

Lord, keep us safe this night,
secure from all our fears.
May angels guard us while we sleep
till morning light appears.

Anon

In darkness and in light,
in trouble and in joy,
help us, heavenly Father,
to trust your love,
to serve your purpose,
and to praise your name;
through Jesus Christ our Lord.

New Patterns for Worship

Jesus Christ is the light of the world:
a light no darkness can quench.

Stay with us, Lord, for it is evening:
and the day is almost over.

Even the darkness is not dark for you:
and the night shines like the day.

Let your light scatter the darkness:
and fill your church with your glory.

cf John 1.5; 8.12; Psalm 139.12; Luke 24.29
New Patterns for Worship

✳

Bedtime Blessing

Heavenly Father,
May your hand of blessing be on ...
   tonight and through tomorrow,
May your everlasting arms uphold them,
May your warm love enfold them,
May they know they are precious and
   honoured in your sight
And that you love them.

Sue Bruce

✳

May God the Father protect you this night,
May God the Son encircle you
   in his loving arms,
May God the Holy Spirit guide you
   throughout the coming day.

Hamish Bruce

✳

Lord, you have brought us through this day
to a time of reflection and rest.
Calm us,
and give us your peace to refresh us.
Keep us close to Christ
that we may be closer to one another
because of his perfect love.
In his name we pray.

New Patterns for Worship

Deep peace of the running wave to you
Deep peace of the flowing air to you
Deep peace of the quiet earth to you
Deep peace of the shining stars to you
Deep peace of the Son of peace to you.

Scots traditional

MILESTONES AND SPECIAL OCCASIONS

We all love those times we celebrate together with our children. We hope the prayers in this section will help as you mark the important events in your child's life. There are also prayers for those milestones that aren't exactly celebrated, but mark a significant change in our role as parents – as our children begin or finish school or prepare to move on. I (Sue) remember crying for hours after my first day at secondary school and saying to my mum 'And I've got to go back every day for five whole years!' It's good to bring moments like this to God. And then there are the holidays – both longed for and dreaded, that can be so wonderful, yet such hard work as well!

Starting School

Father, you know our concerns as parents
today. We place ... in your loving hands
as he takes this big step in his life.
As we thank you for the excitement and
anticipation of this new start, we know
that he will feel new and strange.
We pray that you will surround him with
your love and protection and that the
years ahead may be times of growth in
knowledge and friendship, in confidence
and maturity.
For we pray in your name.
Amen.

Jenny Carrington

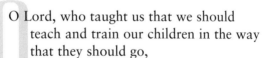

O Lord, who taught us that we should
   teach and train our children in the way
   that they should go,
As we send our children away from us
   to learn,
Be with our children and their teachers.
Amen.

Mary Langshaw

Loving God, please be very close
   to my child on this special day
   as she starts at her new school.
May she feel safe and secure,
may she settle in quickly and make
   new friends,
may she not feel shy or lost or lonely.
Thank you for the knowledge
   that you go with her
and that we can trust her to your safekeeping.
Amen.

Jenny Carrington

First Day at School

Father in heaven,
as ... goes off to school,
inspire me to join those who work tirelessly
for the day when all children
will be able to learn at a school.

Chris Jupp

Heavenly Father,
as ... goes off to school
for the first time,
I pray that you will be with *him/her*,
safe in the knowledge that you will be.
Give ... the strength and self-confidence
to learn to cope with the mistakes,
embarrassments, misunderstandings,
arguments and hurts
that will accompany
the successes, achievements,
revelations, friendships
and joys.

Show me how to support ...
without overdoing it!
I thank you for the early years we've had
and your care that continues as we grow.

Chris Jupp

School Trip, Field Trip

Watch over all who travel today.
We give you the journey and its
    conversations,
Its rest and its thinking time.
We pray for what is studied and learned,
    seen and understood.
May the new landscape and environment
Bring us new awareness
And through the experience nurture
    in each one
A deepening sense of your creation
    and its gift to us.

Hilary Benson

Child's Last Day at Primary School

Dear Jesus
As I move along the road of life, give me
    courage to say goodbye
to the old and welcome the new.
Looking back, thank you for the good
    times at school,
and for the happy memories I can
    never forget.

Thank you that in my times of trouble
you have stayed with me and helped me.
I'm sorry for my arguments with friends.
Please help me not to make the same
    mistakes again.
Looking forward, please help me
    as I go on to secondary school
and leave my old friends.
In both my sadness and my happiness
    help me not to forget the old
but to enjoy the new.
Looking forward, looking back,
    help me Lord Jesus. Amen.

Helen Carrington (aged 11)

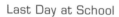

Last Day at School

Lord,
Thank you for the luxury of learning,
the companionship of classes,
the forgiveness of failures,
the stimulus of successes,
the glory of growth,
the feasibilities of the future,
the continuity of your concern
and the lightness of your love.

Chris Jupp

Child Leaving Home

O God our loving Father,
you know with what mixed feelings
    we face the future as ... leaves home.
Thank you for the way he has grown
    and matured
and for helping us to bring him up to take
    this step of independence.
In the weeks and months ahead please lead
    him in the path of goodness and truth,
and protect him from evil.
Thank you that your love for him is greater
    than ours,
and that you have a plan and purpose for
    his life.
We praise you for the privilege of being
    parents
and we ask that you would help us to
    adjust to this change in our role.
Help us not to interfere when it would not
    be helpful,
but to always be ready with our
    unconditional love and support when
    it is needed.

Jenny Carrington

Lord, we praise you for giving ... these
    new opportunities.
Thank you that we know that you will be
    with her to protect from evil
and to guide in the days ahead.
Please show her that your ways give more
    meaning to life
than the endless chasing after selfish goals
    that is so often the way of the world.
Give her strength to stand up for
    Christian values
and not to be afraid to admit to faith
    in you.
Please surround her with your love
and help us always to encourage her
    by our example,
our interest and our prayers.
For we ask in your name.
Amen.

Jenny Carrington

Moving On

Well, Lord, this is it, I suppose:
Our youngest child is eighteen today
Which means all our children are adults –
Theoretically, anyway!

Thank you Lord for the good times –
So much fun and laughter;
Forgive us for the mistakes we made
And the bits we got wrong.

Help us to move on, now, Father
To remember that even though
They will always be our children
They are no longer our responsibility.

Help us to give them space to be themselves
Not to question their decisions
Not to give unwanted advice
Nor ask irritating questions.

Help us hold them in our hearts
    and prayers
Not tied to our apron strings;
Help them to grow up into you
Help us to move on.

Chris Orme

Birthdays

Thank you loving God
for another year to celebrate,
for the chance to be grateful for all we
   have shared with ...
for an excuse to have a party,
for presents and candles and cards
   and cakes,
for the fun we can have with friends
   and family.

Please Lord God,
May today be a special and happy one
   for my child.
May we be reminded afresh of the privilege
   and responsibilities of bringing up
   a child.
May our child ... be safe and protected in
   the coming year.

Sue Bruce

Lord Jesus,
You loved a good party,
Please be with us as we celebrate today.
Thank you for ... and another year
    of their life.
Thank you for being with them,
Please stay close to them today
And guide them through the coming
    months to next year's birthday.

Sue Bruce

Learning to Move On

(A PRAYER FOR A CHILD'S WEDDING DAY)

Lord, thank you for today –
I know now why mothers cry at weddings!

It's not just that the bride looks so beautiful
But the sudden realisation that 'your'
        little girl
Is no longer yours; she's 'his' now,
And even though you love him very much
And are happy about the marriage
Things will never be quite the same again.

Perhaps in life every beginning is also
        an ending:
Every exciting new start for her
Was the end of something special for me.
Slowly she moved away from me, needing
        me less,
Or not in the same way,
But I still need to be needed, Lord!
It's hard to let go.

So now she's married – no – *they're* married.
Help us think 'they', not, 'she', in future.

Help us to stand back and let go,
Not intruding on their relationship,
Not giving advice unless asked,
Not visiting unless invited,
Not taking sides.

Help us to move on,
Supporting them in prayer,
Allowing them to make their own mistakes,
To do things their way, not ours.

Bless them, Lord.

Chris Orme

Holiday Times

We praise you, Father, for the joy
    of holidays,
for the opportunity of visiting new places
    and enjoying different experiences.
Thank you for rest and refreshment and for
    the happy times we can share together.
May we be aware of your presence in the
    wonder of creation
and the beauty of all we see around us.
Help us to be thankful for all that you give
    us to enjoy,
and to return home better able
    to serve you.
For Jesus' sake.
Amen.

Jenny Carrington

For the excitement of packing and leaving
    my home,
Thank you Lord
For the long hot journeys
    in the car/boat/ plane,
Help me Lord
For a warm and comfortable house
    to stay in,
Please Lord
For beaches or mountains or deserts
    or streets,
Thank you Lord
For mosquitoes, danger and rainy days,
Help me Lord
For interesting places to go and to visit,
Please Lord
For swimming pools and tasty food,
Thank you Lord
For packing up and going home,
Help me Lord
For a safe journey home,
Please Lord.
Amen.

Helen Carrington (aged 11)

Christmas Holidays

I'm tired, Lord ...
Was Christmas meant to be like this?
I never stop; there's always more to do:
More presents to wrap, more cards to
    write, more food to buy ...

Help me get it in perspective, Lord
To remember what Christmas is
    really about.
Help me to pace myself
Knowing there's time for everything that
    you want me to do.

Don't let me run round in circles, Lord
Unless you are at the centre;
Help me find just five minutes a day
To be still with you.

Refresh me with loving kindness
And tender mercy – your
Peace and goodwill –
True spirit of Christmas.

Chris Orme

Holiday Times

God, thank you for holidays
For a few weeks of freedom from
     clock-watching,
Lunchboxes, PE kit, reading books,
     shoe bags
And after-school activities.

Help me to enjoy my children's company
To spend time talking and listening
To have fun visiting favourite places
And discovering new ones.

Help them to be co-operative
Willing to share the jobs as well as the joys
Help me to remember to thank them
And to affirm each child each day.

Help us together to remember you –
Lord of all our days; show us yourself
In your wonderful world,
     in each other's faces . . .
May our happiness centre in you!

Chris Orme

IN DIFFICULT TIMES

Despite the happy, smiling faces on the covers of parenting magazines, being a parent is often a painful, scary, heart-breaking experience. In this section we have covered some of those difficult times, such as the on-going worries about non-communication and the tragedies that can occur in parenthood. Sometimes a silent, anguished prayer of 'why, God?' is all we can manage, but we hope these prayers – some written hundreds of years ago and some last year – will help you, your family and friends through these difficult times.

*

It was a tiny thing, my child Lord,
too new to have a name.
And yet it was life Lord, your given life,
the miracle of love.
And now it is over, what pain;
I need your love Lord, to fill
    my aching heart,
your love to counteract that sense of loss.
I can but trust that, as no sparrow falls
unknown to you, my little one will be
    a jewel
that sparkles in your myriad of stars
    cherished by you.
Love never dies Lord, nor those you love.
Hold us now, within your arms,
    secure and safe,
till pain eases and you grant again your
    miracle of life.

Dorothy Pavey

Are you there, God?
Right now it doesn't feel as if you are.
Why, Lord? Why?

You know how much we wanted this baby,
how pleased and excited we were,
getting things ready, thinking about names,
dreaming about the future –
and now there is none.
Or that's how it seems.

I'm aching Lord,
aching in body and spirit,
I've cried till my head aches and I can't cry
    any more.

Help me, Lord.
Comfort me.

Help me to know
not just in my head
but deep down inside me,
that you loved this baby too,
that its life, so short,
was infinitely precious to you
and that our child is now safe,
happy and blessed in your presence.

Chris Orme

As Children Grow Up

Lord, I quickly forget the way it was when
    I was young. If I could remember, I
    might be more patient, more perceptive.
    As it is, I see only 'problems' –
loud music, bizarre hairstyles,
rebellious behaviour, violence,
different moral values.
Forgive me, when that is all I see and when
    I am blind to or ignore everything else –
idealism,
enthusiasm,
commitment,
hard work.
Forgive me, Lord, when I am the 'problem'.

Michael Walker

Father, we pray for young people growing
    up in a difficult and dangerous world.
We pray for those who are unemployed,
who have not worked since they left school
    and have never earned their own money.
We pray for those who are taking their first
    steps in their skill, trade or profession.
We pray for those who feel they have no
    support from the adults around them
and who grow resentful at what they see to
    be their indifference.
We pray for those who are caught up in
    violence either giving it or receiving it.
We pray for those who are morally
    confused and uncertain of what is right
    or wrong.
We pray for young Christians as they strive
    to live out their faith in an
    unsympathetic world.
Father, you are head of all the family.
    Hear our prayers in Jesus' name.

Michael Walker

After an Argument

(A PRAYER FOR PARENTS AND CHILDREN
TO SAY TOGETHER)

Dear Lord Jesus,
We are sorry we got cross with each other
    and argued.
We know it makes you sad when we get
    angry like that.
Please forgive us and help us
    not to do it again.
Amen.

Chris Orme

Lord, may age not make us invulnerable
and certain only of our own rightness.

Michael Walker

I blew it, Lord
and I'm sorry.
It was such a trivial matter
and it could have been sorted out
　　without a slanging match.
Why must I always have the last word – at
　　any price?

Forgive me.
Help me to ask their forgiveness too.
Help me to understand their point of view;
help them to understand mine.
Help them to know I love them
　　even when we disagree.
Help us to grow together in love
　　and understanding
so that discussions don't become arguments
but a genuine sharing of views.

Chris Orme

Heavenly Father,
You are always there to listen,
Whether I'm letting off steam,
Railing against you
Or pleading for help.
Teach me to be like you
And model loving listening.

You are not diminished by listening
    to my curses
Or accusations.
You are next to me, accepting me,
Steady as a rock,
More concerned with my pain
Than your own feelings.

Please send your Holy Spirit to support
    my attempts
To be strong and sensitive
So that I can be
A rock for my child
As the waves break over me.

Chris Jupp

When a Child is Ill

Lord we come to you, like Jairus, for help.
We are worried about our child, what
    might be wrong, how it will turn out.
Also like Jairus it can feel as though you
    are not listening; as though other things
    demand your attention.
There is so little to say, so much to feel.
We pray for faith, for peace
    for the whole family.
Most of all we pray that you give us your
    healing, redeeming grace.
Amen.

Mark Ripley

Prayer for a Child with Special Needs

Lord, *you* gave us this child.
Keep us assured of your faithfulness
    and that you truly love and care.

Lord, you *gave* us this child.
Incline our hearts always to thank you
    for this precious gift.

Lord, you gave *us* this child.
Give us your grace to love and be patient
    even when we feel like giving up.

Lord, you gave us *this child*.
May your goodness and mercy follow him
    all the days of his life
And may he dwell in your house for ever.

Julia Abery

*

Thank you Lord that though
In a few small ways our child may seem
    different from others
In a thousand other ways she is the same.
Thank you for every sense she enjoys.
Thank you for your smile on her.
Thank you that she is made in your image.
Amen.

Mary Langshaw

*

Friends who are Hurt

Dearest God,
the knowledge that some of our friends
    may be being hurt
is more than we can bear.
Show us what we can do
to bring them your love,
your healing
and your concern for their good.

Christopher Herbert

Bullies

Father in heaven, please let your love work
within the hearts of those who bully,
that they may cease from their cruelty
and learn to be at peace with themselves
and with others.

Christopher Herbert

✳

Almighty God, the fountain of all
wisdom, you know our needs before
we ask, and our ignorance in asking; have
compassion on our weakness, and give us
those things which for our unworthiness
we dare not, and for our blindness we
cannot ask, for the sake of your Son,
Jesus Christ our Lord.

Alternative Service Book 1980

✳

Those who are Frightened

O God,
you are filled with tender love
for those who live in fear
– bless all children who live in fear:
afraid of someone at home;
afraid of someone at school;
afraid of a relation;
afraid of someone
    who has treated them wrongly.
Give all those children the wisdom
they need to know whom they can trust,
so that their fears can be heard,
and justice and truth prevail.
And then bring to their wounded minds
    and souls
the healing of your peace.

Christopher Herbert

God give us grace to accept with serenity
    the things that cannot be changed,
courage to change the things that should
    be changed,
and the wisdom to distinguish the one from
    the other.

Reinhold Niebuhr (1892–1971)

＊

Death of a Grandparent

Dear Lord, thank you for grandparents.
My gran was fun.
She used to laugh a lot and read me stories.
She was warm and friendly.
I'll miss her now she's dead.
But I know I'm lucky –
some children never even meet
    their grandparents.
It's funny to think
that one day I'll be old like my gran.
I hope I'll be as smiley and kind as her.
Thank you, Lord, for grandparents.

Christopher Herbert

Teach us, good Lord, to serve thee
   as thou deservest;
to give and not to count the cost;
to fight and not to heed the wounds;
to toil and not to seek for rest;
to labour and not to ask for any reward,
save that of knowing that we do thy will.
Amen.

Ignatius Loyola (1491–1556)

Grant, O Lord, to all those
   who are bearing pain,
thy spirit of healing, thy spirit of life,
thy spirit of peace and hope,
   of courage and endurance.
Cast out from them the spirit of anxiety
   and fear;
grant them perfect confidence and trust
   in thee,
that in thy light they may see light;
through Jesus Christ our Lord.

Anon

Blessed are you, Sovereign God,
     giver of all life;
source of all love, companion in all grief;
you hold all things in life.
You promise that no one can be lost
     from your love
but all will be raised at the last day.
You knew in your body the pain
     of the new creation.
In grieving faith we name you as creator
and praise you as our redeemer,
Father, Son and Holy Spirit.

Rites on the Way

Death of a Child

Loving God,
be with us as we face the mystery of life
    and death.
Strengthen the bonds of our family
    as we bear this loss.
Today we come to you in shock
    and confusion,
help us to find peace in the knowledge of
    your loving mercy to all your children,
and send us your light to guide us
    out of darkness
into the assurance of your love.

A New Zealand Prayer Book

Almighty God, Father of all mercies and
giver of all comfort: deal graciously, we
pray, with those who mourn, that casting
all their care on you, they may know
the consolation of your love; through
Jesus Christ our Lord.
Amen.

Alternative Service Book 1980

DIFFERENT ROLES

*In this section we have included prayers to use
in different roles from that of 'traditional'
parents. These are all written by our family and
friends, based on their own experiences of these
differing roles.*

A Grandmother's Daily Prayer for
her Grandchildren

I pray this day that
God's word will teach you,
God's hand will lead you,
God's wisdom will direct you,
God's power will protect you,
And God's love will surround you.

Rosemary Landreth

Grandparents

I'm a grandparent now Father,
    how strange it seems;
No time at all since the baby in my arms
    was mine.
This baby is a child of my child,
And your child too Father, in many ways
    the same, yet a new person loved
    and welcomed.
Give strength to me Father, to be ready
    when needed, ready to listen to parent
    and child. Keep me listening, hold me
    back from giving continual advice.
I wanted to do it my way, the caring for a
    child, help me to let these parents do it
    their way, but may it be your way too
    Father, that is the best that I can pray,
In Jesus' name.
Amen.

Dorothy Pavey

We pray, Our Father, for grace and
    diligence to understand the needs and
    problems of our grandchildren,
so that we may pray for them effectively
    and enter into their struggles
    as well as their triumphs.
Help us to encourage them and to give
    them praise when they do well,
so that we may forge a bond between us
    that will help them in all the varied
    circumstances of their lives.

Gordon Landreth

✱

We pray, Father, for our grandchildren
    when they are tempted to do wrong,
that they may have the grace and strength
    to resist and choose the right path.
We pray too for them when they have
    fallen into wrongdoing,
that they will be able to acknowledge
    their failure
and know your forgiveness as they seek to
    follow the right way in future.

Gordon Landreth

Dear Father,
I'm going to see ... next week.
It's the first time in a while.
It's always difficult trying to rebuild a
    bit of a relationship during a short visit.
Please help me get on with ...
Help us have fun.
Help us have a good chat.
And help me be an encouragement
    to him/her.
Amen.

Richard Ciencala

Dear Father,
Thank you for my own godparents.
Thank you for their love, their generosity
    and their prayers.
Please help me pass on a part of what they
    gave me to ...
Amen.

Richard Ciencala

Single Parents

Loving God,
There are many reasons why people are
    bringing up children alone,
for those who have painful memories –
    bring healing Lord,
for those who feel lonely – may they know
    your presence,
for those who find it hard to cope – may
    they find support from caring friends,
    neighbours and family,
for those who are fearful – give your
    strength and courage,
for those who feel unloved – may they
    find your love to be sufficient in their
    time of need.

Ali Harper

Prayers from a Single Parent

Lord, sometimes I lie awake at night
    wondering if I am making
    the right decisions,
Wondering if, on my own, I am able
    to do a good job.
Then I remember you are there,
    guiding me with the right answers.
Thank you Lord.

Angela Garnham

＊

Keep me in your presence O Lord.
Guide me and lead me,
In the bringing up of your next generation.
Amen.

Angela Garnham

＊

Adoption and Fostering

We pray for families known to us
    who have adopted, or who are
    intending to adopt children.
We ask for special measures of grace
    and patience,
and rock-solid confidence
    in your good plans for them.
We thank you for the privilege
    of adopting children,
and ask for your love to heal and touch
and bless in the ups and downs
    of making new families.

Pam Macnaughton

*

Loving God,
Thank you for the thousands of foster
  carers in this country who so willingly
  share their homes,
their lives and their families with children
  who cannot live at home.
Father, give them the strength and patience
  they need to face the many challenges
  of this task.
May they find the help they need and may
  they experience fulfilment
as they seek to support these vulnerable
  children.

Ali Harper

*

FAMILY PRAYERS

This final section has a selection of prayers that can be used by parents and children to pray together. From an early age children can be aware of the needs of the world and some of these final prayers, written by people from different countries and cultures, focus on the world-wide family of God.

✳

The Prayer of Parents

O God, you have given us a share
in the creation of new life.
When things go well, may we be thankful;
when we are in despair, comfort us;
when we have lost hope, renew our
    strength;
when we are at peace, cherish us.
And at all times, O God,
fill our hearts with love
for our children, each other and for you.

Christopher Herbert

God bless this house
from roof to floor,
and the door,
God bless us all
for evermore.
God bless the house
with fire and light;
God bless each room
with thy might;
God with thy hand
keep us right;
God be with us
in this dwelling site.

A traditional house blessing

Bless, O God, our families:
give to those who care for us
the spirit of understanding,
    the spirit of love;
that our homes may be places of peace
    and of laughter;
for Jesus' sake.

Christopher Herbert

Loving God
You are Father and Mother to us;
Our life begins in you.
You chose to make your home among us.
You sent your Son to be one with us,
And your Spirit to be with us for ever.
Bless this home
and your people who live here.
Be here today,
as you were yesterday.
Be here tomorrow.
Be our shelter,
our walls to protect us.
Be our windows;
let us see the world through you.
Be our warmth,
to share with all who come in
and all who go forth.

Paul Leingang

The World

O God of grace, forgive us
for building small kingdoms
within our very own lives, families,
careers, small groups,
neighbourhood and country.
Help us to realize that your Kingdom
embraces the whole earth –
the whole universe.

Jane Ella Montenegro, Philippines

*

Great God, you are one God,
and you bring together what is scattered
and mend what is broken.
Unite us with the scattered people of the earth
that we may be one family of your children.
Bind up all our wounds
and heal us in spirit,
that we may be renewed
     as disciples of Jesus Christ,
our Master and Saviour.

New Patterns for Worship

God, what kind of world is this,
That the adult people are going to leave
    for us children?
There is fighting everywhere
And they tell us we live in a time of peace.
You are the only one who can help us.
Lord, give us a new world
In which we can be happy,
In which we can have friends,
And work together for a good future.
A world in which there will not be any
    cruel people
Who seek to destroy us and our world
In so many ways.
Amen.

Prayer from Liberia

To a troubled world
peace from Christ.
To a searching world
love from Christ.
To a waiting world
hope from Christ.

New Patterns for Worship

May the road rise to meet you
May the wind be always at your back
May the sun shine warm upon your face
The rain fall soft upon your fields
And until we meet again
May God hold you
In the hollow of his hands.

Traditional

INDEX OF FIRST LINES

INDEX OF AUTHORS
AND SOURCES

ACKNOWLEDGEMENTS

The compilers and publisher gratefully acknowledge permission to reproduce copyright material in this anthology. Every effort has been made to trace and contact copyright holders. If there are any inadvertent omissions we apologize to those concerned and will ensure that a suitable acknowledgement is made at the next reprint.

The Anglican Church in Aotearoa, New Zealand: material adapted from *A New Zealand Prayer Book – He Karikia Mihinare O Aotearoa*, copyright © The Church of the Province of New Zealand 1989 and used with permission (p. 66).
The Archbishops' Council of the Church of England: from *Common Worship: Services and Prayers for the Church of England*, copyright © 2000 (p. 15); *New Patterns for Worship*, copyright © 2002 (pp. 9, 17, 29, 78, 80); *The Promise of His Glory*, copyright © 1991, 1999 (p. 28) and *Rites on the Way*, copyright © 1998.
Christian Education: from *Further Everyday Prayers* by David Jenkins, Henry McKeating and Michael Walker, copyright © IBRA 1987, used with permission (pp. 6, 53, 54, 55).

Christopher Herbert: from *Pocket Prayers for Children*, Church House Publishing, 1993 and 2004 (pp. 26, 60, 61, 62, 63, 75, 76).

The Revd Rexina Johnson, Sierra Leone (p. 5).

Jane Ella P. Montenegro, United Church of Christ in the Philippines (p. 78).

Westminster John Know Press: from *Daily Prayer: Supplemental Liturgical Resources 5*; used with permission (pp. 32, 78).

The prayer 'God, what kind of world is this' (p. 79) is reproduced with thanks to Clare Amos, USPG, www.uspg.org.uk.